The
United States Presidents

GERALD FORD

ABDO Publishing Company

Megan M. Gunderson

visit us at
www.abdopublishing.com

Published by ABDO Publishing Company, 8000 West 78th Street, Edina, Minnesota 55439.
Copyright © 2009 by Abdo Consulting Group, Inc. International copyrights reserved in all
countries. No part of this book may be reproduced in any form without written permission from the
publisher. The Checkerboard Library™ is a trademark and logo of ABDO Publishing Company.

Printed in the United States.

Cover Photo: Getty Images
Interior Photos: AP Images pp. 12, 19, 20, 28; Corbis pp. 5, 17, 27; Courtesy Gerald R. Ford
    Library pp. 8, 9, 11, 13, 15; Getty Images pp. 23, 26, 29; iStockphoto p. 32;
    National Archives p. 21; White House Photograph Courtesy Gerald R. Ford Library pp. 14, 25

Editor: Heidi M.D. Elston
Art Direction & Cover Design: Neil Klinepier
Interior Design: Neil Klinepier

Library of Congress Cataloging-in-Publication Data

Gunderson, Megan M., 1981-
  Gerald Ford / Megan M. Gunderson.
     p. cm. -- (The United States presidents)
  Includes index.
  ISBN 978-1-60453-451-1
  1. Ford, Gerald R., 1913-2006--Juvenile literature. 2. Presidents--United States--Biography--
Juvenile literature. I. Title.
  E866.G86 2009
  973.925092--dc22
  [B]
                              2008039220

CONTENTS

GERALD FORD

On August 9, 1974, Gerald Ford became the thirty-eighth U.S. president. He had been appointed vice president just eight months before. Ford is the only person to hold both offices without being elected to them.

In high school and college, Ford was a star football player. He then attended law school. After becoming a lawyer, Ford served in the U.S. Navy. He bravely fought in **World War II**. Ford then became a member of the U.S. House of Representatives. There, he had a respected 25-year career.

In 1972, President Richard Nixon and Vice President Spiro T. Agnew were reelected. However, Agnew resigned the following year. President Nixon chose Congressman Ford to replace the vice president. But soon, the Watergate **scandal** forced Nixon to resign. So in 1974, Ford became president.

After taking the oath of office, Ford assured the American people of his leadership. He said, "Our long national nightmare is over."

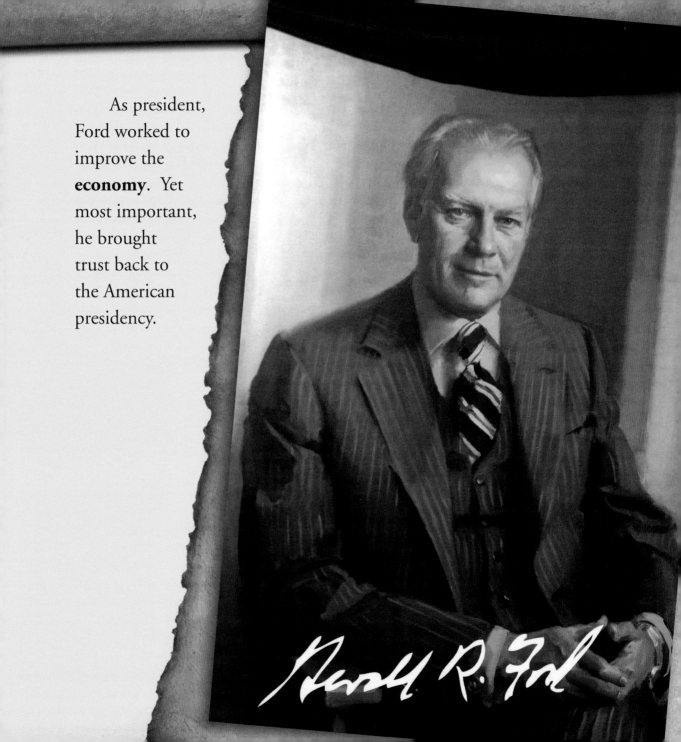

As president, Ford worked to improve the **economy**. Yet most important, he brought trust back to the American presidency.

TIMELINE

1913 - On July 14, Gerald Rudolph Ford Jr. was born in Omaha, Nebraska.

1931 - Ford graduated from Grand Rapids South High School in Grand Rapids, Michigan; Ford began attending the University of Michigan in Ann Arbor, where he became a football star.

1935 - Ford graduated from the University of Michigan; he began working as a coach at Yale University in New Haven, Connecticut.

1941 - Ford graduated from Yale Law School; the United States entered World War II.

1942 - Ford joined the U.S. Navy.

1948 - On October 15, Ford married Elizabeth Anne "Betty" Bloomer; in November, Ford was elected to the U.S. House of Representatives.

1965 - Ford cowrote *Portrait of the Assassin*; he was elected House minority leader.

1973 - On October 10, Vice President Spiro T. Agnew resigned; Ford took the oath to become the new vice president on December 6.

1974 - President Richard Nixon announced his resignation on August 8; on August 9, Ford became the thirty-eighth U.S. president; on December 19, Nelson A. Rockefeller became Ford's vice president.

1975 - In September, Ford survived two assassination attempts.

1976 - Ford ran for president but lost to Jimmy Carter.

1981 - The Gerald R. Ford Library opened; the Gerald R. Ford Museum opened.

1999 - Ford received the Presidential Medal of Freedom.

2006 - On December 26, Gerald Ford died.

While Gerald Ford was president, the United States celebrated its bicentennial. In 1976, 200 years had passed since the signing of the Declaration of Independence.

Donald Rumsfeld served as chief of staff and then secretary of defense under President Ford. Rumsfeld went on to become President George W. Bush's secretary of defense. Ford's next chief of staff, Dick Cheney, became Bush's vice president.

Ford was a lifelong athlete and sports fan. He enjoyed skiing, fishing, and swimming. He also loved tennis, golf, and of course, football.

In 1974, Ford became the first president to visit Japan while in office.

YOUNG JERRY

Gerald Rudolph Ford Jr. was born on July 14, 1913, in Omaha, Nebraska. His parents were Leslie Lynch and Dorothy Gardner King. They originally named him Leslie Lynch King Jr. after his father. But soon, his parents divorced. Then, Dorothy moved with her son to Grand Rapids, Michigan.

Jerry's mother called him "Junie."

In 1916, Dorothy married Gerald R. Ford Sr. He was a paint salesman and a respected community leader in Grand Rapids. Gerald adopted Dorothy's

FAST FACTS

BORN - July 14, 1913

WIFE - Elizabeth Anne "Betty" Bloomer (1918–)

CHILDREN - 4

POLITICAL PARTY - Republican

AGE AT INAUGURATION - 61

YEARS SERVED - 1974–1977

VICE PRESIDENT - Nelson A. Rockefeller

DIED - December 26, 2006, age 93

son and gave him his name. Now, Leslie King Jr. was Gerald Ford Jr. He went by Jerry. Dorothy and Gerald had three more children. Jerry's younger brothers were Thomas, Richard, and James.

In high school, Jerry was a good student. He did well in history and government. And, he was popular with his classmates. Jerry was also a star on the football team. Jerry graduated from Grand Rapids South High School in 1931.

Young Jerry

STAR FOOTBALL PLAYER

Jerry's football talent earned him a **scholarship**. In 1931, he began attending the University of Michigan in Ann Arbor. He played center on Michigan's football team. In 1932 and 1933, the team went undefeated and won national championships.

In 1934, Jerry was voted the team's most valuable player. This honor earned him a place in two important games the following year. He played in the East-West College All-Star game. Then, he played in the Chicago Tribune College All-Star game.

At Michigan, Jerry also worked hard on his schoolwork. He studied **economics** and **political science**. And, he served on the student council. Jerry graduated near the top of his class in 1935.

The Green Bay Packers and the Detroit Lions wanted Jerry to play for them. But he decided not to play professional football. Instead, Jerry chose to coach sports and become a lawyer.

As a football player, Jerry learned teamwork and discipline. This later helped him succeed in politics.

LAW AND WAR

In 1935, Ford began working at Yale University in New Haven, Connecticut. He coached football and boxing. Three years later, he began attending Yale Law School.

While in school, Ford supported **Republican** Wendell Willkie's 1940 presidential campaign. **Democrat** Franklin D. Roosevelt defeated Willkie in the election. Yet, Ford had learned much about politics.

Ford graduated from law school in 1941. He then returned to Grand Rapids. There, Ford opened a law firm with his friend Philip Buchen. He also became politically active.

Philip Buchen served as a White House lawyer during Ford's presidency.

Later that year, the United States entered **World War II**. So in 1942, Ford joined the U.S. Navy. He served nearly four years in the navy. Ford earned many honors. He rose to the rank of lieutenant commander.

Ford returned to Michigan in 1946. There, he continued his law practice. Yet Ford also began thinking about running for public office.

In the navy, Ford served as an assistant navigation officer aboard the USS Monterey.

POLITICS AND FAMILY

The Ford family

On June 17, 1948, Ford announced his decision to run for the U.S. House of Representatives. He spoke well during the campaign. He also listened to the concerns of voters, which voters liked.

Ford easily defeated his opponent, **Democrat** Fred J. Barr Jr. That November, Ford won more than 74,000 votes. Barr earned just under 47,000.

14

Meanwhile, Ford had started a family. On October 15, 1948, Ford had married Elizabeth Anne "Betty" Bloomer. Betty had grown up in Grand Rapids. As a young woman, she studied dance in New York. Later, she returned to Grand Rapids to work in fashion and teach dance.

The Fords had three sons and one daughter. Michael was born in 1950. John followed in 1952. Then in 1956, Steven was born. The Fords welcomed their daughter, Susan, in 1957.

After the 1948 election, the Fords moved to Washington, D.C.

CONGRESSMAN FORD

In Washington, D.C., Ford studied the ways of Congress. He followed **debates** and learned how to get laws passed. Congressman Ford paid attention to the people he represented. He also compromised with his opponents. Ford became known as a hardworking, honest congressman.

Michigan voters liked Ford's actions in the House. They reelected him 12 times! Each time, Ford won by at least 60 percent of the vote.

From 1951 to 1965, Congressman Ford served on the House Appropriations Committee. This group of representatives oversees government spending.

On November 22, 1963, President John F. Kennedy was **assassinated**. Then, new president Lyndon B. Johnson named Ford to the Warren Commission. This group investigated the assassination.

Congressman Ford (left) with members of the Warren Commission

In Congress, Ford voted against expanding the power of the national government. He voted to limit labor union power and minimum wage increases.

Ford also voted for two bills that protected African Americans. The **Civil Rights** Act passed in 1964. The Voting Rights Act became law the next year.

In 1965, there were more **Democrats** than **Republicans** in the House of Representatives. This meant the Republicans were in the minority.

That year, Ford challenged **minority leader** Charles A. Halleck for his position. Ford won 73 votes to Halleck's 67. So, Ford became the new House minority leader. He held this position until 1973.

Ford had a good attendance record in Congress. Yet, he often traveled the country in support of other Republicans. Each year, Ford made nearly 200 speeches during his trips. In 1966, Ford's speeches helped his party win 47 more seats in the House.

In 1970, Ford led an attempt to **impeach** U.S. **Supreme Court justice** William O. Douglas. Ford felt Douglas had misused his position as a judge. The attempt failed. As a result, Congressman Ford's reputation suffered. Luckily, he soon recovered.

Representative Richard Nixon (left) *welcomed Ford to Congress. Nixon introduced himself right after Ford took the oath to join the House. The two future presidents soon became friends.*

Ford wanted to continue advancing in the House. He desired to become **Speaker of the House**. To do that, there had to be more **Republicans** than **Democrats** in the House. But the Republicans did not expect this to happen soon. So, Ford decided that the 1974 election would be his last. Yet Ford's plans were about to change.

APPOINTED LEADER

Spiro T. Agnew was the second vice president in U.S. history to resign. The first was John C. Calhoun in 1832.

In 1973, President Richard Nixon faced a challenging situation. Vice President Spiro T. Agnew was accused of taking bribes. He also admitted to lying on his income taxes. On October 10, Agnew resigned.

Now, President Nixon had to nominate a new vice president. Nixon and his advisers felt Congressman Ford was the best choice.

The House and the Senate must approve a nominated vice president. The Senate voted 92 to 3 in favor of Ford. The House approved Ford with a vote of 387 to 35.

HOUSE OF REPRESENTATIVES
WASHINGTON, D. C. 20515

GERALD R. FORD
MINORITY LEADER

October 11, 1973

Dear Mr. President:

On the basis of the criteria outlined by you at the meeting in your office I am recommending the following in the order of my preference:

1. John Connally
2. Mel Laird
3. Nelson Rockefeller or Ronald Reagan

I will not go into the reasons for my views as I'm sure you are familiar with reasons in each instance.

You can rest assured that I will fully cooperate and assist in this and all other problems in the months ahead.

Warmest personal regards.

Sincerely,

Gerald R. Ford, M. C.

The President
The White House

On December 6, 1973, Ford took the oath of office in the House chamber. It was the first time a U.S. vice president had not been elected to office.

Vice President Ford quickly got to work. He made appearances across the country in support of the **Republican** Party. Ford traveled more than 100,000 miles (160,000 km) in less than eight months!

At President Nixon's request, Ford and other congressmen presented suggestions for a new vice president.

Meanwhile, President Nixon's involvement in a **scandal** was becoming public. In 1972, burglars had broken into the Watergate building in Washington, D.C. **Republicans** had wanted information from the **Democratic National Committee** headquarters. People then began covering up White House involvement in the break-in. This incident is called the Watergate scandal.

President Nixon denied his involvement in the cover-up. But he was unable to clear his name. On August 8, 1974, Nixon announced he would resign. Now, Vice President Ford would become president.

Ford became the thirty-eighth U.S. president on August 9. He called on all Americans to try to move past Watergate. "Our long national nightmare is over," he said. "Our **Constitution** works. Our great republic is a government of laws and not of men."

On September 8, President Ford pardoned Nixon. This meant that Nixon could never be sent to jail for his Watergate crimes.

Ford believed that pardoning Nixon would help the country move on. Instead, it angered many Americans. They wanted Nixon punished for what he had done. After the pardon, Ford's popularity dropped.

Meanwhile, Ford named New York governor Nelson A. Rockefeller as his vice president. Rockefeller took office on December 19. Now, neither the president nor the vice president had been elected by the people. This was another first in U.S. history!

Nelson A. Rockefeller (left) *with Ford*

PRESIDENT FORD

President Ford quickly turned his attention to the **economy**. Many people were out of work. Prices for goods and services were rising fast. The country also had a shortage of oil and gas.

Ford asked Congress to cut taxes. He also held down government spending. Soon, more Americans were back at work. Prices were still high, but they were not rising as fast. Business was improving.

The United States was also dealing with the end of the **Vietnam War**. During the war, many young men had not wanted to fight. Some had left the country to avoid military service. Ford decided to pardon them in return for two years of public service. Again, many Americans were unhappy with Ford's decision.

In April 1975, Ford ordered the last U.S. forces out of Vietnam. At the same time,

SUPREME COURT APPOINTMENT

JOHN PAUL STEVENS - 1975

24

thousands of Vietnamese were evacuated. More than 100,000 of them settled in the United States.

Then in May, Cambodia captured a U.S. cargo ship and 39 crew members. Ford knew America needed to look strong after the **Vietnam War**. So, he sent U.S. Marines to rescue the captives. They succeeded, but 41 lives were lost. Still, Ford was praised for his decision. His popularity began to rise.

In September 1975, Ford faced two **assassination** attempts. On September 5, Ford was in California to give a speech. There, a woman named Lynette "Squeaky" Fromme pointed a gun at him. She was caught before she

Ford and Dole lost the 1976 election by fewer than 2 million popular votes.

could harm the president. Fromme was sentenced to life in prison.

Then on September 22, Sarah Jane Moore shot at Ford outside a California hotel. Again, Ford was unhurt. Moore was caught and sentenced to life in prison. In 2007, she was released.

The year 1976 brought another election. Ford hoped Americans would give him a chance to continue leading the country. On August 18, the **Republican** Party nominated Ford to run for president.

President Ford chose Kansas senator Bob Dole as his **running mate**. The **Democrats** chose Jimmy Carter to run for president. His running mate was Minnesota senator Walter Mondale. Ford campaigned hard. However, Carter won the election. He received 297 electoral votes to Ford's 240.

PRESIDENT FORD'S CABINET

AUGUST 9, 1974–
JANUARY 20, 1977

- **STATE –** Henry A. Kissinger
- **TREASURY –** William E. Simon
- **DEFENSE –** James R. Schlesinger
  Donald Rumsfeld (from November 20, 1975)
- **ATTORNEY GENERAL –** William B. Saxbe
  Edward H. Levi (from February 7, 1975)
- **INTERIOR –** Rogers C.B. Morton Jr.
  Stanley K. Hathaway (from June 13, 1975)
  Thomas S. Kleppe (from October 17, 1975)
- **AGRICULTURE –** Earl L. Butz
  John A. Knebel (from November 4, 1976)
- **COMMERCE –** Frederick B. Dent
  Rogers C.B. Morton Jr. (from May 1, 1975)
  Elliot L. Richardson (from February 2, 1976)
- **LABOR –** Peter J. Brennan
  John T. Dunlop (from March 18, 1975)
  Willie J. Usery Jr. (from February 10, 1976)
- **HEALTH, EDUCATION, AND WELFARE –**
  Caspar W. Weinberger
  F. David Matthews (from August 8, 1975)
- **HOUSING AND URBAN DEVELOPMENT –**
  James T. Lynn
  Carla Anderson Hills (from March 10, 1975)
- **TRANSPORTATION –** Claude S. Brinegar
  William T. Coleman Jr. (from March 7, 1975)

RETIREMENT

Ford left the White House in January 1977. President Carter thanked Ford "for all he has done to heal our land." Ford had become president at a difficult time. He had done an honorable job as the nation's leader.

The Fords retired to Rancho Mirage, California. Ford remained highly respected. In 1980, Ronald Reagan was running for president. He asked Ford to be his **running mate**. Ford did not run. However, he continued to support the **Republican** Party. That year, Reagan was elected president.

Ronald Reagan (right) *served as president from 1981 to 1989.*

In 1981, the Gerald R. Ford Library opened in Ann Arbor. The same year, the Gerald R. Ford Museum opened in Grand Rapids. In 1999, Ford received the Presidential Medal of Freedom. This award honored his public service and his leadership after Watergate.

Gerald Ford died in Rancho Mirage on December 26, 2006. He remains the only person to become vice president and president without being elected. Ford is remembered for bringing honor and pride back to the White House.

President and Mrs. Clinton honored Ford with the Presidential Medal of Freedom.

OFFICE OF THE PRESIDENT

BRANCHES OF GOVERNMENT

The U.S. government is divided into three branches. They are the executive, legislative, and judicial branches. This division is called a separation of powers. Each branch has some power over the others. This is called a system of checks and balances.

EXECUTIVE BRANCH

The executive branch enforces laws. It is made up of the president, the vice president, and the president's cabinet. The president represents the United States around the world. He or she oversees relations with other countries and signs treaties. The president signs bills into law and appoints officials and federal judges. He or she also leads the military and manages government workers.

LEGISLATIVE BRANCH

The legislative branch makes laws, maintains the military, and regulates trade. It also has the power to declare war. This branch consists of the Senate and the House of Representatives. Together, these two houses make up Congress. Each state has two senators. A state's population determines the number of representatives it has.

JUDICIAL BRANCH

The judicial branch interprets laws. It consists of district courts, courts of appeals, and the Supreme Court. District courts try cases. If a person disagrees with a trial's outcome, he or she may appeal. If the courts of appeals support the ruling, a person may appeal to the Supreme Court. The Supreme Court also makes sure that laws follow the U.S. Constitution.

QUALIFICATIONS FOR OFFICE

To be president, a person must meet three requirements. A candidate must be at least 35 years old and a natural-born U.S. citizen. He or she must also have lived in the United States for at least 14 years.

ELECTORAL COLLEGE

The U.S. presidential election is an indirect election. Voters from each state choose electors to represent them in the Electoral College. The number of electors from each state is based on population. Each elector has one electoral vote. Electors are pledged to cast their vote for the candidate who receives the highest number of popular votes in their state. A candidate must receive the majority of Electoral College votes to win.

TERM OF OFFICE

Each president may be elected to two four-year terms. Sometimes, a president may only be elected once. This happens if he or she served more than two years of the previous president's term.

The presidential election is held on the Tuesday after the first Monday in November. The president is sworn in on January 20 of the following year. At that time, he or she takes the oath of office:

I do solemnly swear (or affirm) that I will faithfully execute the office of President of the United States, and will to the best of my ability, preserve, protect and defend the Constitution of the United States.

LINE OF SUCCESSION

The Presidential Succession Act of 1947 defines who becomes president if the president cannot serve. The vice president is first in the line of succession. Next are the Speaker of the House and the President Pro Tempore of the Senate. If none of these individuals is able to serve, the office falls to the president's cabinet members. They would take office in the order in which each department was created:

Secretary of State

Secretary of the Treasury

Secretary of Defense

Attorney General

Secretary of the Interior

Secretary of Agriculture

Secretary of Commerce

Secretary of Labor

Secretary of Health and Human Services

Secretary of Housing and Urban Development

Secretary of Transportation

Secretary of Energy

Secretary of Education

Secretary of Veterans Affairs

Secretary of Homeland Security

BENEFITS

• While in office, the president receives a salary of $400,000 each year. He or she lives in the White House and has 24-hour Secret Service protection.

• The president may travel on a Boeing 747 jet called Air Force One. The airplane can accommodate 70 passengers. It has kitchens, a dining room, sleeping areas, and a conference room. It also has fully equipped offices with the latest communications systems. Air Force One can fly halfway around the world before needing to refuel. It can even refuel in flight!

• If the president wishes to travel by car, he or she uses Cadillac One. Cadillac One is a Cadillac Deville. It has been modified with heavy armor and communications systems. The president takes Cadillac One along when visiting other countries if secure transportation will be needed.

• The president also travels on a helicopter called Marine One. Like the presidential car, Marine One accompanies the president when traveling abroad if necessary.

• Sometimes, the president needs to get away and relax with family and friends. Camp David is the official presidential retreat. It is located in the cool, wooded mountains in Maryland. The U.S. Navy maintains the retreat, and the U.S. Marine Corps keeps it secure. The camp offers swimming, tennis, golf, and hiking.

• When the president leaves office, he or she receives Secret Service protection for ten more years. He or she also receives a yearly pension of $191,300 and funding for office space, supplies, and staff.

PRESIDENTS AND THEIR TERMS

PRESIDENT	PARTY	TOOK OFFICE	LEFT OFFICE	TERMS SERVED	VICE PRESIDENT
George Washington	None	April 30, 1789	March 4, 1797	Two	John Adams
John Adams	Federalist	March 4, 1797	March 4, 1801	One	Thomas Jefferson
Thomas Jefferson	Democratic-Republican	March 4, 1801	March 4, 1809	Two	Aaron Burr, George Clinton
James Madison	Democratic-Republican	March 4, 1809	March 4, 1817	Two	George Clinton, Elbridge Gerry
James Monroe	Democratic-Republican	March 4, 1817	March 4, 1825	Two	Daniel D. Tompkins
John Quincy Adams	Democratic-Republican	March 4, 1825	March 4, 1829	One	John C. Calhoun
Andrew Jackson	Democrat	March 4, 1829	March 4, 1837	Two	John C. Calhoun, Martin Van Buren
Martin Van Buren	Democrat	March 4, 1837	March 4, 1841	One	Richard M. Johnson
William H. Harrison	Whig	March 4, 1841	April 4, 1841	Died During First Term	John Tyler
John Tyler	Whig	April 6, 1841	March 4, 1845	Completed Harrison's Term	Office Vacant
James K. Polk	Democrat	March 4, 1845	March 4, 1849	One	George M. Dallas
Zachary Taylor	Whig	March 5, 1849	July 9, 1850	Died During First Term	Millard Fillmore

PRESIDENT	PARTY	TOOK OFFICE	LEFT OFFICE	TERMS SERVED	VICE PRESIDENT
Millard Fillmore	Whig	July 10, 1850	March 4, 1853	Completed Taylor's Term	Office Vacant
Franklin Pierce	Democrat	March 4, 1853	March 4, 1857	One	William R.D. King
James Buchanan	Democrat	March 4, 1857	March 4, 1861	One	John C. Breckinridge
Abraham Lincoln	Republican	March 4, 1861	April 15, 1865	Served One Term, Died During Second Term	Hannibal Hamlin, Andrew Johnson
Andrew Johnson	Democrat	April 15, 1865	March 4, 1869	Completed Lincoln's Second Term	Office Vacant
Ulysses S. Grant	Republican	March 4, 1869	March 4, 1877	Two	Schuyler Colfax, Henry Wilson
Rutherford B. Hayes	Republican	March 3, 1877	March 4, 1881	One	William A. Wheeler
James A. Garfield	Republican	March 4, 1881	September 19, 1881	Died During First Term	Chester Arthur
Chester Arthur	Republican	September 20, 1881	March 4, 1885	Completed Garfield's Term	Office Vacant
Grover Cleveland	Democrat	March 4, 1885	March 4, 1889	One	Thomas A. Hendricks
Benjamin Harrison	Republican	March 4, 1889	March 4, 1893	One	Levi P. Morton
Grover Cleveland	Democrat	March 4, 1893	March 4, 1897	One	Adlai E. Stevenson
William McKinley	Republican	March 4, 1897	September 14, 1901	Served One Term, Died During Second Term	Garret A. Hobart, Theodore Roosevelt

PRESIDENT	PARTY	TOOK OFFICE	LEFT OFFICE	TERMS SERVED	VICE PRESIDENT
Theodore Roosevelt	Republican	September 14, 1901	March 4, 1909	Completed McKinley's Second Term, Served One Term	Office Vacant, Charles Fairbanks
William Taft	Republican	March 4, 1909	March 4, 1913	One	James S. Sherman
Woodrow Wilson	Democrat	March 4, 1913	March 4, 1921	Two	Thomas R. Marshall
Warren G. Harding	Republican	March 4, 1921	August 2, 1923	Died During First Term	Calvin Coolidge
Calvin Coolidge	Republican	August 3, 1923	March 4, 1929	Completed Harding's Term, Served One Term	Office Vacant, Charles Dawes
Herbert Hoover	Republican	March 4, 1929	March 4, 1933	One	Charles Curtis
Franklin D. Roosevelt	Democrat	March 4, 1933	April 12, 1945	Served Three Terms, Died During Fourth Term	John Nance Garner, Henry A. Wallace, Harry S. Truman
Harry S. Truman	Democrat	April 12, 1945	January 20, 1953	Completed Roosevelt's Fourth Term, Served One Term	Office Vacant, Alben Barkley
Dwight D. Eisenhower	Republican	January 20, 1953	January 20, 1961	Two	Richard Nixon
John F. Kennedy	Democrat	January 20, 1961	November 22, 1963	Died During First Term	Lyndon B. Johnson
Lyndon B. Johnson	Democrat	November 22, 1963	January 20, 1969	Completed Kennedy's Term, Served One Term	Office Vacant, Hubert H. Humphrey
Richard Nixon	Republican	January 20, 1969	August 9, 1974	Completed First Term, Resigned During Second Term	Spiro T. Agnew, Gerald Ford

PRESIDENTS 26–37, 1901–1974

PRESIDENT	PARTY	TOOK OFFICE	LEFT OFFICE	TERMS SERVED	VICE PRESIDENT
Gerald Ford	Republican	August 9, 1974	January 20, 1977	Completed Nixon's Second Term	Nelson A. Rockefeller
Jimmy Carter	Democrat	January 20, 1977	January 20, 1981	One	Walter Mondale
Ronald Reagan	Republican	January 20, 1981	January 20, 1989	Two	George H.W. Bush
George H.W. Bush	Republican	January 20, 1989	January 20, 1993	One	Dan Quayle
Bill Clinton	Democrat	January 20, 1993	January 20, 2001	Two	Al Gore
George W. Bush	Republican	January 20, 2001	January 20, 2009	Two	Dick Cheney
Barack Obama	Democrat	January 20, 2009			Joe Biden

"Freedom is always worth fighting for." Gerald Ford

WRITE TO THE PRESIDENT

You may write to the president at:

**The White House
1600 Pennsylvania Avenue NW
Washington, DC 20500**

You may e-mail the president at:

comments@whitehouse.gov

GLOSSARY

assassinate - to murder a very important person, usually for political reasons.

civil rights - the individual rights of a citizen, such as the right to vote or freedom of speech.

Constitution - the laws that govern the United States.

debate - a contest in which two sides argue for or against something.

Democrat - a member of the Democratic political party. Democrats believe in social change and strong government.

Democratic National Committee - a group that provides leadership for the Democratic Party.

economy - the way a nation uses its money, goods, and natural resources. Economics is the science of this.

impeach - to charge a public official with misconduct in office.

justice - a judge on the U.S. Supreme Court.

minority leader - the leader of a party that does not have the greatest number of votes in a legislative body, such as the U.S. House of Representatives.

political science - the study of government and politics.

Republican - a member of the Republican political party. Republicans are conservative and believe in small government.

running mate - a candidate running for a lower-rank position on an election ticket, especially the candidate for vice president.

scandal - an action that shocks people and disgraces those connected with it.

scholarship - a gift of money to help a student pay for instruction.

Speaker of the House - the highest-ranking member of the party with the majority in Congress.

Supreme Court - the highest, most powerful court in the United States.

Vietnam War - from 1957 to 1975. A long, failed attempt by the United States to stop North Vietnam from taking over South Vietnam.

World War II - from 1939 to 1945, fought in Europe, Asia, and Africa. Great Britain, France, the United States, the Soviet Union, and their allies were on one side. Germany, Italy, Japan, and their allies were on the other side.

WEB SITES

To learn more about Gerald Ford, visit ABDO Publishing Company on the World Wide Web at **www.abdopublishing.com**. Web sites about Gerald Ford are featured on our Book Links page. These links are routinely monitored and updated to provide the most current information available.

INDEX